SPORTS GREAT
DARRYL
STRAWBERRY

—*Sports Great Books*—

BASEBALL

Sports Great Jim Abbott
0-89490-395-0/ Savage

Sports Great Barry Bonds
0-89490-595-3/ Sullivan

Sports Great Bobby Bonilla
0-89490-417-5/ Knapp

Sports Great Orel Hershiser
0-89490-389-6/ Knapp

Sports Great Bo Jackson
0-89490-281-4/ Knapp

Sports Great Greg Maddux
0-89490-873-1/ Thornley

Sports Great Kirby Puckett
0-89490-392-6/ Aaseng

Sports Great Cal Ripken, Jr.
0-89490-387-X/ Macnow

Sports Great Nolan Ryan
0-89490-394-2/ Lace

Sports Great Darryl Strawberry
0-89490-291-1/ Torres & Sullivan

BASKETBALL

**Sports Great Charles Barkley
(Revised)**
0-7660-1004-X/ Macnow

Sports Great Larry Bird
0-89490-368-3/ Kavanagh

Sports Great Muggsy Bogues
0-89490-876-6/ Rekela

Sports Great Patrick Ewing
0-89490-369-1/ Kavanagh

Sports Great Anfernee Hardaway
0-89490-758-1/ Rekela

**Sports Great Magic Johnson
(Revised and Expanded)**
0-89490-348-9/ Haskins

**Sports Great Michael Jordan
(Revised)**
0-89490-978-9/ Aaseng

Sports Great Jason Kidd
0-7660-1001-5/ Torres

Sports Great Karl Malone
0-89490-599-6/ Savage

Sports Great Reggie Miller
0-89490-874-X/ Thornley

Sports Great Alonzo Mourning
0-89490-875-8/ Fortunato

Sports Great Hakeem Olajuwon
0-89490-372-1/ Knapp

**Sports Great Shaquille O'Neal
(Revised)**
0-7660-1003-1/ Sullivan

Sports Great Scottie Pippen
0-89490-755-7/ Bjarkman

**Sports Great David Robinson
(Revised)**
0-7660-1077-5/ Aaseng

Sports Great Dennis Rodman
0-89490-759-X/ Thornley

Sports Great John Stockton
0-89490-598-8/ Aaseng

Sports Great Isiah Thomas
0-89490-374-8/ Knapp

Sports Great Dominique Wilkins
0-89490-754-9/ Bjarkman

FOOTBALL

Sports Great Troy Aikman
0-89490-593-7/ Macnow

Sports Great Jerome Bettis
0-89490-872-3/Majewski

Sports Great John Elway
0-89490-282-2/ Fox

Sports Great Brett Favre
0-7660-1000-7/ Savage

Sports Great Jim Kelly
0-89490-670-4/ Harrington

Sports Great Joe Montana
0-89490-371-3/ Kavanagh

Sports Great Jerry Rice
0-89490-419-1/ Dickey

Sports Great Barry Sanders
0-89490-418-3/ Knapp

Sports Great Emmitt Smith
0-7660-1002-3/ Grabowski

Sports Great Herschel Walker
0-89490-207-5/ Benagh

HOCKEY

Sports Great Wayne Gretzky
0-89490-757-3/ Rappoport

Sports Great Mario Lemieux
0-89490-596-1/ Knapp

Sports Great Eric Lindros
0-89490-871-5/ Rappoport

TENNIS

Sports Great Steffi Graf
0-89490-597-X/ Knapp

Sports Great Pete Sampras
0-89490-756-5/ Sherrow

SPORTS GREAT DARRYL STRAWBERRY

John Albert Torres
and
Michael John Sullivan

—Sports Great Books—

Enslow Publishers, Inc.

40 Industrial Road	PO Box 38
Box 398	Aldershot
Berkeley Heights, NJ 07922	Hants GU12 6BP
USA	UK

http://www.enslow.com

Library of Congress Cataloging-in-Publication Data:

Torres, John Albert
    Sports Great Darryl Strawberry / by John Albert Torres and Michael John Sullivan.
      p. cm. — (Sports great books)
    Summary: Follows the life and career of the baseball player who was named
Rookie of the Year in the National League in 1983.
    ISBN 0-89490-291-1
    1. Strawberry, Darryl—Juvenile literature. 2. Baseball players—United
States—Biography—Juvenile literature. [1. Strawberry, Darryl. 2. Baseball players.
3. Afro-Americans—Biography.]
    I. Sullivan, Michael John, 1960–   . II. Title. III. Series.
GV865.S87T67   1990
92–dc20
[796.357'092]   89-28918
[B]   CIP
                                       AC

Printed in the United States of America

10 9 8 7 6

To Our Readers:
All Internet addresses in this book were active and appropriate when we went to press. Any
comments or suggestions can be sent by e-mail to Comments@enslow.com or to the
address on the back cover.

Illustration Credits: AP/Wide World Photos, pp. 18, 60; Bob Olen/*New York Post*,
p. 46; Ray Stubblebine/*New York Post*, p. 48; Nancy Richmond, pp. 9, 11, 13, 17,
21, 22, 25, 27, 29, 32, 34, 37, 40, 43, 44, 52, 56.

Cover Photo: AP/Wide World Photos.

Contents

Chapter 1

It was a cold, damp night at Shea Stadium in Flushing, New York, just east of New York City. The Mets fans were draped with winter coats, colorful scarves, and woolen gloves. The players' breath looked like smoke because of the cold. The fall night in Flushing gave the national television audience the feeling that snow was in the air.

The New York Mets were holding a slim 6–5 advantage against the Boston Red Sox in Game 7 of the 1986 World Series. The Red Sox had rallied for two runs in the top of the eighth, and there were worried faces in the New York dugout and in the stands.

The momentum seemed to shift to the Red Sox, and the Mets desperately needed more offense. Coming to bat was New York slugger Darryl Strawberry. The Mets right fielder had struggled at the plate thus far in the World Series against Boston—Darryl was batting just .174 for the series. A roar from the crowd greeted Strawberry as he planted himself in the batter's box 60 feet 6 inches away from the Red Sox hurler.

The first pitch from the Red Sox right-handed pitcher Al Nipper was a fastball. Strawberry swung late and popped it foul into the third base stands. Nipper again challenged Darryl with a fastball. Darryl, with his eyes glued to the spin of the ball, was not late this time. He hit the ball, but it bounced sharply to Mets first base coach Bill Robinson. Darryl now had a problem. He had two strikes, and Nipper had a chance to make the "Straw Man," as Strawberry is called, go after a bad pitch. The batter's job now was to protect the plate. Strawberry rose to the challenge. Nipper turned and spun toward the plate with a curveball. It didn't fool Darryl. Strawberry drove the ball skyward through the cold night air. The ball landed beyond the right center field fence, a blast of over 420 feet, giving the Mets a lift and ending Boston's momentum. Even more important, it gave New York a much needed insurance run. (An insurance run provides a team with at least a two-run lead. It makes it harder for the opposing team to catch up.)

The spirit of the Mets was lifted as the crowd of 55,032 screamed its approval for its young superstar. Coach Robinson greeted Darryl with a high-five as he rounded first base. The cheers rose from section to section as his right spike shoe touched second.

The song "New York, New York" played from the Shea Stadium speakers as Darryl stepped on third and received congratulations from then third base coach Buddy Harrelson. It was a glorious celebration for Darryl as he entered the happy Mets dugout.

The fans continued to scream their love for Strawberry. They wanted to salute Darryl once more. He pleased the roaring crowd and came out of the dugout. He raised his eyes to the sky and lifted his arms in triumph as the roar became deafening.

A long drive energizes Darryl's legs towards first.

It was the run the Mets needed. Darryl finally had delivered a big hit. The Mets scored again in the eighth inning for an 8–5 lead. Only three outs separated the Mets from becoming world champions.

In the Boston ninth inning, Mets relief pitcher Jesse Orosco got the first two Boston players out. Orosco recorded the final out on a strikeout against Boston second baseman Marty Barrett. And so the Mets capped their spectacular season with the World Championship. As the fans rushed onto the field to mob their heroes, Darryl glided in from right field with a satisfied smile on his face. His team had won the championship, and he had made a contribution.

"We needed a big run to give us a lift," a grinning Strawberry said during the victory celebration. "It felt good to get a hold of one." It was a rewarding season for Darryl. He and the Mets achieved the toughest accomplishment in major league baseball.

The Mets had anticipated that Darryl would someday become a superstar when they drafted him as the first pick overall in the 1980 June amateur draft. Darryl was still in high school, but major league scouts were impressed with his great talent. The Mets knew about Strawberry and so did the other twenty-five major league teams.

Darryl batted .400 and belted five homers in his senior year at Crenshaw High School in Los Angeles. Darryl, an all-around athlete, also starred in basketball and helped Crenshaw capture a city championship. He was also the quarterback of the football team. Darryl received many scholarship offers from colleges and universities to play either basketball or baseball. The Mets were happy he chose to play baseball with them. In fact, he received a $210,000 signing bonus with his first professional contract.

What impressed the Mets most was Strawberry's power

Darryl Strawberry gets ready to face the Boston Red Sox.

and speed—a rare and valuable combination in any sport. At 6-feet, 6-inches, and 195 pounds, Darryl displayed his exceptional speed by stealing thirty-six bases in 1987. Strawberry also demonstrated awesome strength with his bat, belting thirty-nine home runs and thirty-two doubles, accumulating 104 runs batted in (RBI). (A run batted in is when a run scores because of a hit, walk, ground out, fly out, or a hit by pitch.) Darryl has hammered many tape-measure homers and often is compared to New York Yankees legend and Hall of Famer Mickey Mantle. Mantle, considered one of baseball's greatest players, starred for the Yankees during the 1950s and 1960s. He was known for his ability to hit tape-measure home runs. (A tape-measure home run is a term used for a home run that travels a very long distance, usually more than 450 feet.) Mantle collected 536 home runs during his career.

There is no better example of Darryl's bat speed and power than his performance on opening day of the 1988 season. The Mets were in Montreal, Canada, playing the Montreal Expos and owned a comfortable 7–2 lead. Darryl had already belted his first homer of the season. It was the seventh inning, and Expos hurler Randy St. Claire was on the mound. St. Claire made a terrible mistake by throwing an inside fastball to Strawberry. Darryl swung and launched the ball high toward right field. Before Darryl could touch first base, the ball rocketed off the concrete rim surrounding the Olympic Stadium roof.

Many of the Mets and Expos players said it was the longest home run they had ever seen. Some scientists estimated the ball would have travelled 525 feet if it had not struck the concrete rim.

"I thought it was going through the roof," Montreal Manager Buck Rodgers said. "That's the longest home run

Darryl is ready to make the catch.

I've seen in my 32 years in the game. And I've seen Mickey Mantle, Roger Maris, Harmon Killebrew, and Reggie Jackson." Darryl, despite his mammoth moon shot, remained humble and concentrated on team goals. "It was just another home run," he said. "I'm more of a team player. I'm not concerned with how far my homers go."

Darryl also has a strong and accurate arm. Opposing baserunners rarely dare to test Darryl's arm when the ball comes to him in right field. "Darryl has one of the best throwing arms in the league," Cincinnati Reds outfielder and longtime friend Eric Davis said.

Darryl's former high school teammate and major league player Chris Brown agrees. "He's got a great arm. In high school, he would pitch and play center field. He had the best arm on the team."

Strawberry's athletic skills have never been questioned. He has a unique blend of speed, power, and agility in the outfield. However, developing that raw potential into super-stardom has not been easy for the Straw Man.

The early years were, at times, a rough battle for Darryl on and off the field. Darryl, like many of us, faced challenges, but he knew it would take hard work and time to develop as a person and a player. He has journeyed a long way to realize his potential and, despite some disappointments, has become a superstar.

Chapter 2

The New York Mets became a major league team in 1962. That same year, Darryl was born to Ruby Strawberry on March 12th in Los Angeles, California. He was a healthy boy who enjoyed playing basketball, baseball, and football. As a child, Darryl was always encouraged by his mother to participate in all athletic activities. She also insisted that Darryl devote enough time to his studies. However, it was not until his high school days that Darryl became serious about sports.

It was also during his teenage years that Darryl met future Detroit Tiger Chris Brown. The competition between the two made them better players. "We became close friends when we were in high school," Brown said. "He was always a good athlete. He might have been able to play professional basketball, too."

Darryl has learned that hard work can help make dreams come true. He learned this from his number one fan and inspiration, his mom Ruby.

"My mom taught me that sometimes you have to grow up fast. I just go out on the field and have fun. Those are the good things you learn about yourself." Ruby also taught Darryl that when you have a job to do, it is better not to count on anyone but yourself.

Darryl has learned a special skill. He has learned to hit against left-handed pitchers as well as he hits against right-handers. He practiced by facing many lefties in batting practice and in games. Left-handed sluggers usually have trouble hitting against left-handed pitchers. This is because the power hitter takes a very big swing and may be fooled by the pitcher's motion. Most left-handers throw across their bodies unlike right-handed pitchers who throw straight from the top of their delivery. When Darryl first joined the Mets, he had a tough time batting against left-handers.

Darryl's early talent also created an unusual burden. From a young age, Darryl was the center of attention. While he was still in high school, Darryl appeared on the cover of *Sports Illustrated*, the most visible sports magazine in the country. He was chosen to appear in *Sports Illustrated* because he was considered to be the best amateur baseball player in the United States. Thanks to the support of Darryl's family and friends, young Darryl didn't succumb to the media pressure that has brought down many bright young stars before him.

"You have to understand one thing about Darryl," Mets pitcher Bobby Ojeda told *The Sporting News*, "he has grown up in the sports pages where everything he has done has been blown up. That must have been tough on him."

Darryl's high school basketball coach, Willie West, remembers well the first time he saw Darryl walk on the basketball court. "He was a tall, skinny kid," West recalled. "He was already the starting quarterback on the football team and was also a great baseball player. He didn't play basketball

16

Darryl joins his teammates for a dugout view of the game.

Darryl was an outstanding pitcher and outfielder for Crenshaw High School in Los Angeles.

until his junior year at Crenshaw but as soon as I saw him on the court, I was impressed."

West had seen many athletes with good physical skills walk the halls of Crenshaw High School, but something about Darryl separated him from the others. "What I noticed about Darryl was that he was very confident in his abilities. He was very aggressive. He knew he had the ability and he also knew that he could accomplish just about anything he wanted to in sports," West said.

During his senior year at Crenshaw, Darryl became the starting forward and led the team to the city championship. His excellence on the basketball court prompted him to wonder whether his future was in basketball or baseball.

Darryl often dreamed of throwing down tremendous slam dunks for the Los Angeles Lakers in the championship game of the National Basketball Association finals. He also dreamed of hitting home runs for the Los Angeles Dodgers. Darryl was approached by dozens of scouts and colleges who tried to sway him from one sport to another. Finally, after talking about his future with his mother, Darryl decided to play baseball. "Darryl could have probably played professional basketball," West said. "He had the height and the skills. But I think he made the right choice to go with baseball. He was much more aggressive on the baseball field than on any other field of play."

Although West never met Darryl's mother, he knew that she was the calming influence in his life. The ghettos around Crenshaw High School in Los Angeles often destroyed the future of many young people. But Darryl's mother never let her son fall into that trap.

To this day, Darryl feels extra pressure to perform well when the Mets travel to Los Angeles. His mother is always in the stands watching when the Mets play in Dodger Stadium.

Darryl only batted .213 at Dodger Stadium during his first five seasons in the major leagues. He hit three home runs and had only thirteen RBI. (Batting averages are calculated by dividing the number of hits by the number of at-bats. When a batter walks or is hit by a pitch, it does not count as a time at bat. A .300 batting average means that the batter succeeds with three hits in every ten at-bats.)

Darryl has his own personal rooting section in Dodger Stadium when his family and friends cheer him on. While Darryl appreciates the fan support, their expectations sometimes make him try too hard. "I do tend to press when we go to Los Angeles," Darryl said. "I have to stay within myself and just concentrate on playing to the best of my abilities."

Darryl is not alone. Many athletes find it difficult to perform well in their hometowns. Darryl's former teammate and Mets co-captain Keith Hernandez has always had trouble playing in front of his father in his hometown, San Francisco. During one six-year stretch as a Met, Hernandez, a lifetime .300 hitter, batted only .266 while playing in Candlestick Park. Hernandez has also managed only three home runs and thirteen RBI—Darryl's identical numbers in Los Angeles.

It may be for the best that Darryl plays most of his home games in New York, about 3,000 miles away from his Los Angeles home. Although there are many great pressures in playing in the Big Apple, they seem small in comparison to trying to impress Mom.

Darryl was not the only athlete in his family. He has two brothers that were also good baseball players. His brother Michael played minor league baseball in the Dodgers farm system. Another brother, Ronnie, played college baseball in California.

Being blessed with such awesome talent and being called a superstar at such a young age presented Darryl with yet

When Darryl needs confidence, he thinks of his mother.

Life in the major leagues can be filled with pressure.

another obstacle that he had to overcome. How does a youngster whom everyone agrees will be a superstar ballplayer stay motivated? For inspiration, Darryl remembers the lesson his mother taught him: work hard.

"She always finds a way to remind me," Darryl said. Darryl finds motivation and inspiration in his mother's example. She raised five children and had to do it mostly on her own since Darryl's father left home when Darryl was only thirteen.

"I get my confidence from her," Darryl says. "She's always been a confident person. With five kids and being alone she was always confident. She was always teaching us to be confident and to believe in ourselves. When I go back home I realize that I have been playing baseball my whole life and I did not arrive to where I am at by being a dog at it. It takes a lot of hard work. I spend the off-seasons thinking about my future, why I'm here, and what I can do with the talent I was blessed with."

"The future is limitless for Darryl Strawberry," said former Mets batting coach Jim Frey. "He has the ability to do great things. His future will depend on how his motivation will carry him."

Major-league pitcher Bill Gullickson agrees: "The sky is the limit for Darryl, if he stays motivated."

Darryl has come a long way from his days as a three-sport athlete at Crenshaw High School and the ghettos lining its borders. He has also struggled with his mother and his four brothers and sisters to get by. But some dreams just never die. The major leagues seemed far away then, but now they are real.

And if Darryl ever feels unmotivated or uninspired—or if he should ever forget what it took for him to become a great baseball player—his mother will be sure to remind him.

Chapter 3

Darryl had completed the first step. He played well in high school and was drafted by a major league team. But that was only the beginning. First, he had to climb through the various levels of the minor leagues before he could play for the parent club, the New York Mets.

Minor leagues provide a system for major league teams to develop their young talent. Young players usually start out playing single-A ball. As they become better ballplayers, they are promoted to the double-A level and then to triple-A. Triple-A is one step below the major leagues.

Many people picture the life of a professional ballplayer as being very glamorous: first class airlines, fancy hotels, thousands of adoring fans, and media exposure. What most people do not know is that life in the minor leagues can be anything but glamorous. Airlines? Fancy hotels? Fans? The minor leagues usually mean long bus rides, small towns, and empty stadiums. But it was in the minor leagues that Darryl Strawberry perfected his skills and prepared himself for the big leagues.

Darryl shows a lot of hustle on the field.

"Darryl probably never had to take playing baseball seriously before," former Mets batting coach Jim Frey said. "He was so good at it that he just relied on his talents. He learned that in order to make the major leagues, and in order to be successful he would have to take everything—even practice—seriously."

Darryl did not go to college. He went straight from the baseball fields of Crenshaw High School to the outfield of the Kingsport (Tennessee) Mets in the Appalachian League in 1980. The Appalachian League is the lowest level of A baseball in the minor leagues. Darryl, as he had done in the past, made it look so easy. He lined a single to center in his first professional at-bat. From there, Darryl steamrolled his way through the minor leagues. His minor league totals and statistics record a great beginning. Throughout his minor league career, Darryl got better as the competition got better. He improved steadily until he was finally called up to the majors in 1983.

When Darryl first came up to the Mets, people viewed him as a savior. In 1976, the Mets had won eighty-six games and finished in third place. But the Mets struggled and suffered through seven consecutive losing seasons. During that time, the New York Yankees appeared in four World Series, won five division titles, and won the majority of New York baseball fans' hearts. The Mets needed someone to spark the team and bring hope back to Mets fans. Darryl was that spark.

"When I was a rookie, I came up and got into all the media hype and pressure of playing in New York. I had communication problems with my teammates and the pitchers were a lot tougher than I thought they would be," Darryl told *The New York Times*. Still, Darryl proceeded to win the National League Rookie of the Year Award after his first big league season. His talent was obvious, but he still had lots of skills that needed to be developed.

During his first four seasons, Darryl averaged twenty-seven runs and eighty-six RBI. While those were great achievements for most power hitters, the fans in New York wanted more from the Straw Man.

Darryl glides down to first base after a single.

But as he became more confident in his abilities, Darryl started to perform like everyone expected. He started to win the respect and admiration of his teammates and the fans.

"There is no question that Darryl has always had the ability. But now, his intensity is incredible," Met infielder Tim Teufel said.

Former Mets outfielder Mookie Wilson was a member of the Mets before Darryl's arrival and was a witness to Darryl's evolution from a good player to a dominating player. "Darryl was very rebellious during his first few seasons," Wilson told *The Sporting News*. "If things didn't go his way, he'd talk about quitting and going home. That was youth talking. I think he realized that this was the real world and not some high school fantasy. I think one day he woke up and said, 'I'm 25 years old and I'm acting like an 18-year-old.' Once he realized that, he was on his way to the greatness we all expected of him when we first saw him play." And greatness did follow.

The 1986 baseball season can be seen as the turning point in Darryl's career. It seemed that everything worked for Darryl that year, and he finally reached the higher levels of play in the major leagues. On April 30, 1986, Darryl collected the first five-hit game of his career when he hit three singles, a double, and a homer against the Atlanta Braves.

In 1986, the Mets finished in first place in the Eastern Division, 21-1/2 games ahead of the second-place Philadephia Phillies. The Houston Astros won the Western Division and were set to face the Mets in a best-of-seven-games series. The winner of these playoffs would advance to the World Series against the winner of the American League playoffs.

In the 1986 playoffs against the Astros, Darryl led all players with two home runs and five RBI. One of his swings

Darryl steadies himself for another visit to the plate.

may have saved the Mets from going down three games to two against their rivals from Texas.

In the fifth game of the playoffs, the Mets were losing 1–0 in the fifth inning. They were facing ageless flamethrower Nolan Ryan. Ryan, who was thirty-nine years old at the time, is known for having one of the best fastballs in all of baseball. His fastball, nicknamed the "Ryan Express," was once clocked by the radar gun at 101 miles per hour. (The radar gun is a device used by coaches and major league scouts to determine how fast a pitcher is throwing.) Ryan had held the Mets to one infield single during the first four innings of this game. He was using his blazing fastball and slow curveball to paralyze the Mets' bats.

Darryl connected on Ryan's first pitch of the fifth inning to crush a line drive homer just inside the right field foul pole. The Mets did not manage another hit against Ryan. The score was tied 1–1 at the end of nine innings. The Mets finally won the game in the twelfth inning against reliever Charlie Kerfeld. If it had not been for Darryl's home run, the game might never have gone to extra innings, and the Mets could have lost.

The Mets went on to win the sixth game and eventually defeated the Boston Red Sox in the World Series.

"He's a great player. That's all there is to it," Keith Hernandez said. "Jack Clark [San Diego Padres] and Darryl are the two most feared hitters in the league." Darryl has not only evolved into a feared hitter and fine fielder but has finally inherited the leadership role he sought when he was younger. In 1984, Darryl embarrassed himself and his teammates when he brazenly said, "I want to be the leader of this team." The older Met players did not like the young player's attitude.

In 1988, a more mature Strawberry claimed: "I am not the leader of this team. All I can do is bust my tail on the field and try to help this club win. That's all I want. Winning means more to me than anything."

"He's a leader on the field," Teufel said. "He has taken charge. We all see that. He's dedicated to winning. I think that kind of rubs off."

Darryl's name is consistently near the top of major league offensive leaders, and he has become an All Star. He has broken or is approaching most Met offensive records. It took a little longer than most fans expected, but Darryl Strawberry is now one of the best players in baseball.

"I'm just happy that everyone was willing to wait," Darryl said. "It was just a matter of time before I began to do what I know I'm capable of doing. I didn't know until recently how good I could be. But, I also know that I'm not as good as I can be."

Can Darryl get much better? Darryl averaged 31 homers and 91 RBI in his first six major league seasons. If he keeps up that pace for twenty seasons, Darryl will have around 620 home runs and 1,820 RBI. Those kinds of numbers would rank Strawberry with some of the best players ever to play baseball.

Discussing statistics and greatness sometimes embarrasses Darryl. "I don't want to think about things like that. It's way too early in my career. I want to take it one game at a time. I just want to go out there and play hard every game."

It's clear to see how Darryl has improved every season in the major leagues. He is a team leader, a great hitter, and good fielder. No matter how good a season Darryl and the Mets have, he always promises to try a little bit harder the following season.

Darryl has always been one of the Mets' top base stealers.

Chapter 4

When Darryl Strawberry was called up to the major leagues there were a lot of people waiting for him at Shea Stadium. Not all of them were fans, but most of them were admirers. There were photographers and reporters stirring behind home plate. A podium was set up for the arrival of Darryl. The rookie outfielder, called up on May 4, 1983, from the Mets triple-A farm club in Tidewater, Virginia, instantly received fame because of his name. The Tidewater Tides is a team in the International League—one of the highest levels of competition in triple-A baseball. People involved in baseball knew about Darryl because of the way he had hit the ball in the minor leagues.

Photographers clicked away, and reporters scribbled in notebooks. Darryl showed his enthusiasm and desire to remain in the major leagues.

"I was surprised to be called up this soon," Strawberry said at the May 6th press conference. "I was just trying to do my job there [at Tidewater]. But my big day is coming true, I'm going to play at Shea Stadium."

Strawberry's arrival could not have come at a better time for New York Mets fans. Their once-proud team had lost its claim as New York City's best team to the New York Yankees. The Yankees had played in four World Series in the last ten years and won two. The Mets had not played in the series since 1973. Met fans were becoming impatient. Shea

Darryl drives one out of the ballpark.

Stadium seats were empty while fans poured into Yankee Stadium in record numbers.

Mets fans were treated to a glimpse of Darryl's ability in spring training of 1983. Strawberry wowed them with his power at the plate and skill on the base paths. Darryl had an exceptional spring and was selected as the winner of the Johnny Murphy Award. This award is given to the Mets top rookie in training camp.

Strawberry was still sent down to Tidewater in an effort not to rush him into the majors. Hopefully, he would gain another season of valuable experience in the minors. "Under ideal circumstances, we still prefer he stay down," Mets General Manager Frank Cashen told *The New York Times*.

At batting practice three hours before his first game as a Met, Darryl put in motion his long arms and looping swing that made him famous in Los Angeles. He drove the small white baseball into the swirling wind and over the Shea Stadium outfield fences. With each sky-bound blast, photographers used their film, and reporters and fans enjoyed the flight of Strawberry's drives.

Members of the media were comparing Strawberry's arrival to the time when a man named Willie Mays was called up by the New York Giants of the National League on May 25, 1951. Willie Mays was a Hall-of-Fame slugger for the New York (now San Francisco) Giants. He played for the Mets in 1973, his last season. Darryl reminded the media of Mays because both had exceptional power, great speed, and tremendous throwing ability. Mays belted 660 home runs during his career and is third on the all-time home run list. "I'm not familiar with the things Willie has done," Darryl said. "I'm just Darryl Strawberry and I have to play like me. I know I have the talent to play, but it's not going to be easy.

I'm going to have my ups and downs, and I have got to be able to deal with them."

There were 15,916 in attendance for Darryl's major league debut. Mets officials said that about 3,500 came to see Strawberry. Cincinnati Reds pitcher Mario Soto held Darryl hitless in four at-bats, striking out Strawberry three times. But the game was extended into extra innings when the score remained tied after nine innings.

Darryl came to bat in the eleventh inning and faced Reds right-hander Tom Hume. Hume tried to slip a fastball past the nervous rookie. Strawberry swung hard, and the crowd at Shea Stadium leaped to their feet in unison as the ball soared toward the right field foul pole. But there was no victory lap for Darryl. The ball hooked foul by only a couple of feet. Darryl reached base on a walk.

Darryl batted again in the thirteenth inning and once again patiently worked out a walk and then stole second. He scored a three-run homer by then-Met George Foster. "I didn't contribute with the bat, but I hope I helped the club anyway," Strawberry said after the Mets 7–4 victory.

"I was pleased with the fans' reaction. They've waited a long time to see me." But it was worth the wait for the fans who have followed Strawberry since his minor league days in Kingsport, Tennessee.

"In his first year there," Cashen told *The New York Times*, "people from all around were flying in to see him after they found out where Kingsport was. I don't remember anyone coming up to the majors with this kind of attention. That's why I talked to him in a brief but intense conversation. I told him not to go shouldering the burden. The danger is that Darryl will think he has to do it."

Strawberry handled the pressure of the New York City

Darryl tries to concentrate on the game.

fans and media with his bat. In his twenty-seventh major league at-bat, he slammed his first major league homer, a drive off Pittsburgh Pirates pitcher Lee Tunnell on May 16th.

The next evening, Strawberry unloaded on San Diego Padres pitcher Tim Lollar at Shea Stadium. Darryl's three-run blast led the Mets to a 6–4 victory. But Darryl struggled through his first twenty-four games in the major leagues, hitting only .161 with three homers and nine RBI. There were reporters in the media wondering if the Mets had called him up from the minors too soon.

But Strawberry's bat speed seemed to quicken, and his concentration at the plate appeared to sharpen. In Darryl's final ninety-eight games, he batted .282 with twenty-three homers and sixty-five RBI. Strawberry collected his first two-homer game, slamming two long drives off St. Louis pitcher Bob Forsch on June 28th. Darryl had answered the critics with his bat and pleased the New York fans.

The accomplishments in Strawberry's first major league season promised the Mets a brighter future. Darryl finished his rookie year with twenty-six homers and seventy-four RBI, both New York records for any Mets rookies. Both of those totals led the National League for rookies.

"I can't say that I expected him to do that well," Frank Cashen said. "But I was not surprised that he accomplished some of the things he did in his rookie year."

Strawberry's first year performance earned him the respect of the Baseball Writers Association of America, who voted him the 1983 Rookie of the Year. The Baseball Writers Association votes for the player that it feels was the best rookie during the season.

Strawberry received eighteen of a possible twenty-four first place votes and was the only player selected on all twenty-four ballots. Darryl complied 106 points to 49 for runner-up Craig McMurtry, a pitcher for the Atlanta Braves.

"His winning the award helps the club more than anything we can do," said Mets President Fred Wilpon. "It's more than anything we can do other than developing into a contender. It's the most effective kind of marketing—Darryl has become a very popular kind of figure and when he does well it affects the whole organization in a positive way."

"I am an organization man," Darryl told *The Sporting News*. "I think the organization needed this. It's showing something bright for the New York Mets future."

Strawberry's rise as a superstar also added more pressure to perform for himself and his team. There was much expected of Darryl Strawberry when he made his debut in the majors, and he satisfied the critics. The hardest part was beginning for Darryl and the Mets. Expectations were increased—both were expected to perform better.

Darryl gets another base hit.

Chapter 5

The Mets battled the Chicago Cubs for the 1984 National League East title until the last week of the season. The Cubs ended up winning the division by 6-1/2 games. Darryl and the Mets looked forward to 1985 spring training with high hopes. The Mets had acquired All Star catcher Gary Carter and young slugger Howard Johnson to help Darryl with the offense.

One of the problems facing Darryl that year was his tendency to get depressed when he fell into a batting slump. Sometimes the slump would affect his play on the field, too.

"He began to get down on himself," Mets Manager Davey Johnson told United Press International. "It was something he hadn't encountered before. I probably would have kept him in the minors a little while longer but they brought him up here. Playing in New York and being put on every magazine cover in the world—that's tough. I had to take him aside and talk with him . . . and you've got to watch how you handle these situations because the rest of the players are watching every move you make."

The Mets got off to a flying start in 1985. Darryl was a major factor in the Mets winning five straight games. Darryl's homer in the ninth inning defeated the Reds 2–1 in the fourth game of the season. Four games later, Darryl's homer sparked a 10–6 victory over Pittsburgh. The following week, Darryl's home run helped the Mets defeat the St. Louis Cardinals 7–6.

The Mets were winning, and Darryl was tearing the cover off the ball—life seemed great. But during the third inning of a game against the Philadelphia Phillies, Darryl made a diving catch off a line drive, by then-Philadelphia second baseman Juan Samuel. Darryl landed on his right hand and tore a ligament in his thumb. Two days later, Darryl had his hand operated on at St. Luke's-Roosevelt Hospital in Manhattan. Darryl could not play baseball for seven weeks.

In the first nine days Darryl's bat was missing from the Mets lineup, New York did not score a run in three games. In the seven weeks Darryl was on the disabled list, the Mets won only twenty games and lost twenty-three.

When Darryl returned to the Mets lineup, he had to wear a fiberglass shield and elastic band on his right hand. He wore these protective measures because if his hand had been hit with a baseball while batting, the tender thumb could have been re-injured. By then, the Mets had stumbled into third place. Everyone had surely found out how important Darryl was to the team.

With Darryl back in the lineup, the Mets won twenty-seven of their next thirty-eight games. At that amazing pace, the Mets moved back into first place in the National League East. Darryl contributed ten homers and thirty-two RBI. Former Mets player Hubie Brooks told United Press International, "If the game's on the line, he's lethal. He can hit the ball out of any part of the ballpark. The Mets can't win

Darryl talks to former coach Bill Robinson about strategy.

Helping out the team is more important than keeping the uniform clean.

without Darryl. When he was hurt, they lost. When he came back, they won."

The Mets slumped and found themselves in second place by 2-1/2 games at the All Star break. Despite missing seven weeks, Darryl was selected to the National League All Star team. Darryl made his teammates and his fans proud. He helped the National League to a 6–1 victory over the American League. Darryl scored twice and made two outstanding defensive plays in right field.

Darryl immediately helped the Mets get a good start in the second half of the 1985 season. Darryl drove in nine runs and hit two homers to lead the Mets to three victories in four games against the Atlanta Braves. St. Louis was then in first place. On August 4 the Mets trailed the Cards by only a half-game. But a players strike was set for August 6th. Darryl put the Mets back into first place on August 5th when he homered three times and drove in five runs to spark a Mets 7–2 victory over the Cubs in Chicago. Darryl was happy with his performance but sad about the future. "It's a shame to have a day like this and know that you may be on strike tomorrow," Darryl said.

The players did go on strike, but an agreement brought baseball back to the field on August 8th. The two-day break did not affect Darryl, and he promptly hit a home run to ignite a New York 14–7 victory over the Montreal Expos. "I'm different this year," Darryl told United Press International. "I'm more relaxed. I'm coming to the ballpark ready to play, mentally. Not letting things bother me on the field and off. I've been here nearly three years and something has happened each year to make it hard . . . . This year, just when I thought things were straightened out, I got hurt. But the injury was a blessing. It gave me a chance to sit and watch the pitchers and

Darryl, his wife Lisa, and son Darryl, Jr., view a Knicks basketball game.

hitters. Watching made me a better hitter when I came back. The injury made me a better player and a better man."

It also made the 1985 Mets a better team. Darryl drove in four runs and hit a homer to help the Mets defeat the San Francisco Giants 7–0 on August 24th. The Mets led the Cardinals by a half game, but on August 23rd they lost a doubleheader to the San Diego Padres. The Mets were not destined to catch the Cardinals, but it was a great year for Darryl. Despite missing seven weeks, he hit twenty-nine homers and drove in seventy-nine runs. One of those homers was a game-winning blast against St. Louis on October 1st during the first game of a crucial series. After Darryl was re-activated following his injury, the Mets compiled a 60–33 record.

"His talent sets him apart," pitcher Bill Gullickson said. "He is a young hitter who has veteran judgement. You never see him over-swing. He knows the strike zone and hits the pitch. The sky is the limit if he stays motivated."

Darryl did stay motivated throughout the 1985 season. When it mattered most, in the final month of the season (September), Darryl hit nine homers and drove in thirty runs.

In 1985, Darryl matured into the ballplayer most people thought he would become. It was a big year for Darryl. He signed a five-year contract worth one million dollars a year. It meant financial stability to Darryl, his new wife Lisa, and his newborn son Darryl, Jr. It also motivated Darryl in some ways about his off-the-field responsibilities. "Being married, plus having a son, made me more relaxed, gave me more to go on," Darryl said.

But Darryl, Jr., is not the only important kid now in the Straw Man's life. One day, Darryl took time to visit sick children at the Ronald McDonald House in New York City. Ronald McDonald House is where very ill children and their parents can stay while getting medical treatment. Darryl spent a couple of hours talking, signing autographs, and handing out Met baseball caps to these children. When Darryl left, the children's smiles lit up the room. Darryl left with a big smile on his face, too.

"There's a lot more to life than just hitting home runs. I

Darryl takes time out to talk with kids.

really enjoy being with the kids," he said. Spending time off the field trying to help others is nothing new to Darryl. He spends his winters playing charity basketball games in California. The games raise money to help educate young people about the dangers of drugs. Joining Darryl on the court are his friends Detroit Tiger Chris Brown, San Diego Padre Tony Gwynn, Cincinnati Red Eric Davis, and San Francisco Giant Kevin Mitchell.

"We talked to the young people about how drugs are all around us. We have to do something about it. Anytime we can help somebody and do something good it leaves you with a great feeling," Darryl said.

"In '84 or '85 I started playing basketball with Darryl and it's something that has carried over to every winter. Darryl really cares about young kids," Eric Davis said.

In January of 1987, a United Press International release reported that Darryl and his wife Lisa separated. That fall, Darryl and Lisa got back together. While Darryl continued to mature as a father and husband, he dedicated more and more of his time to needy children. For example, he became involved with the Give-A-Wish Foundation, which grants wishes to very sick children.

Midway through the 1988 baseball season, Darryl also had to find time for another important child. He became a father for the second time when his daughter, Diamond Nicole, was born. Young people had become a special part of Darryl's life.

Chapter 6

"He's Superman." St. Louis Cardinal Manager Whitey Herzog is outspoken when praising Darryl Strawberry. Herzog became a believer after Darryl smashed St. Louis pitching with two mammoth home runs on June 15, 1988. But the Cardinal pitchers were at a disadvantage. They did not know that Darryl had made a promise before the game. He made a promise to his son Darryl, Jr., that he would hit a home run for him on his third birthday. Darryl did more than that. He doubled his gift.

Darryl erased a 1–0 Cardinal lead in the bottom of the first inning when he sent a Chris Carpenter fastball into the seats in right field for a three-run homer. Former Mets Wally Backman and Lee Mazzilli scored ahead of him.

In Darryl's next at-bat, he crushed another Carpenter fastball into the Mets bullpen in right field giving New York a 4–1 advantage. It was his seventeenth multiple home run game, and the Mets went on to win.

"This is my kid's birthday and I promised him I would hit

a home run for him," Darryl said after the game. "He's always talking about hitting home runs. You can ask his mommy."

The home runs were even more important because the Mets were without first baseman and team captain Keith Hernandez, who was on the disabled list. Gary Carter and Kevin McReynolds, who were in slumps, also did not play.

Darryl hit thirty-nine home runs in 1988. However, to be able to sacrifice oneself for the team is even more important than trying to hit home runs. In 1988, Darryl became a better team player. Sacrificing his power to move a runner to scoring position is a good example of Darryl becoming a better player. In May of 1988, Darryl sacrificed himself and helped the Mets defeat the San Diego Padres.

Darryl was facing left-hander Mark Davis, who is considered one of the toughest left-handers in the National League. There was no score in the game in the tenth inning. There were no outs, and Keith Hernandez was on second base. Darryl knew that it was his job to move the runner to third base, so he grounded a nasty curve ball to second base, allowing Hernandez to go to third. Hernandez then scored on a wild pitch, and the Mets won the game 1–0. Although it is not counted as a sacrifice in the stats, Darryl chose not to go after the big hit and instead concentrated on moving the runner over to third. His ability to sacrifice his great power helped the Mets win an important game.

Darryl will not only sacrifice himself for the team, he will stand up and defend his teammates. In Cincinnati, Reds pitcher Tom Browning hit Mets second baseman Tim Teufel with a pitch. Darryl charged the mound to get at Browning. Darryl also issued a warning to Browning and to other pitchers in the league who might try to hit his teammates.

Darryl is a protective father off the field and an equally protective "father" on the field, but he realizes that fighting is not the answer. "When I get hit my first reaction is to hit back. It's wrong," Darryl said.

It is important for a leader to lead by example, stick by his teammates, and show them that they have a friend. But, during 1988 spring training, some Mets teammates wondered if Darryl was their friend.

Although he is a left-handed batter, Darryl can hit well against both right- and left-handed pitchers.

In an article written by New York sportswriter Mike Lupica that appeared in *Esquire* magazine during spring training in 1988, Darryl criticized his teammates and manager for their performances in 1987. The 1987 Mets finished in second place in the Eastern Division of the National League behind the St. Louis Cardinals. His teammates, manager, the media, and the fans were disappointed in Darryl after the article was published. But the bad feelings seemed to be gone on opening day in Montreal when Darryl slammed two homers. The second blast was the home run that bounced off the concrete rim of Olympic Stadium in Montreal.

Players, coaches, and fans rejoiced in Darryl's fast start. "When he gets his bat going, he is one of the top batters in baseball," Mets Manager Davey Johnson said. "He is so strong. When he gets into a groove he can be awesome."

Darryl, a left-handed batter, had as much success against left-handed pitching as he did with pitchers hurling from the right side. It was July 3, 1988. Mookie Wilson, a Met outfielder, was at second base, and Darryl stepped up to the plate. On the mound for the Houston Astros was left-handed pitcher Bob Knepper, considered one of the top southpaws in the National League. Strawberry and Knepper battled to a 2–2 count. Knepper tried to strike out Darryl with his best pitch—a curve ball. Strawberry jumped on the spinning ball and smashed it off the facade in right field for his twentieth homer of the year.

Strawberry continued to pound the ball until the month of August when he went into a slump. Except for this month, Darryl carried the Mets with his offensive power. During this stretch, first baseman Keith Hernandez was injured for two months, and left fielder Kevin McReynolds was slumping. Darryl was a one-man offensive show. He was the main reason why the Mets held off the Pittsburgh Pirates for the National League East championship.

Despite slumping in August, the Mets slugger led the National League with thirty-nine homers and 101 RBI. Darryl batted .269 and scored 101 runs. With the Straw Man's effort, the Mets raced past the Pirates and captured their second division championship in three years. Only the Los Angeles Dodgers stood between the Mets and another World Series. Many expected New York to be there.

The Mets took a two-game-to-one lead in the National League Championship series. Game 4 was played on a mild fall night at Shea Stadium. Mets fans anticipated another triumph and expected another World Series visit. However, the Dodgers were not going to quit. They took a 2–0 advantage behind excellent left-hander John Tudor. With Keith Hernandez on first, Darryl stepped up to the plate. Like Mickey Mantle of the Yankees arriving to the plate in the 1950s and 1960s, the cheers slowly rose for the fans' most valuable player.

The roar grew as Darryl's bat crushed a Tudor fastball. The ball landed in the Mets bullpen to tie the score at 2–2. Ignited by Strawberry's homer, Met left fielder Kevin McReynolds drilled another Tudor pitch over the left field wall for a 3–2 New York advantage. Mets ace Dwight Gooden carried a 4–2 lead into the ninth inning. It appeared that New York was about to take a commanding 3–1 lead in the series. It did not happen.

Gooden walked outfielder John Shelby and surrendered a game-tying home run to Dodgers catcher Mike Scioscia. The Mets never recovered and lost the game in extra innings. The Dodgers defeated the Mets in seven games. Darryl was as sad as anyone. "We had our opportunities to beat them," he said.

"But, give them credit, they came back and battled. But we battled too; it hurts."

Despite the unhappy finish to the season for Darryl and the Mets, it was still rewarding for Strawberry. On August 2, Darryl had compiled a .291 batting average and belted twenty-nine home runs with seventy-three RBI. But his slump in August was one factor that hurt him in the race for the Most Valuable Player (MVP) in the National League.

The season hurt even more when the National League announced their MVP on November 15th. It was Kirk Gibson of the Los Angeles Dodgers. "Kirk Gibson had an outstanding year," Darryl told the *New York Post.* "I have no reason to be down about anything. I'm just going to continue to do better, set my standards higher. One day I'll be appreciated."

Gibson's statistics were surpassed by Darryl's. Gibson batted .290 with fourteen fewer home runs and twenty-five less RBI than Darryl. However, the Dodger outfielder did score 106 runs and provided Los Angeles with positive leadership.

"My average hurt me a lot," Darryl told the *Post.* But all I can do is have a better year next year. "

"It's always nice to get a lot of attention when it's well deserved and it was well deserved by Kirk," Darryl told *New York Newsday.* "But when you do have big numbers that should be part of the game. People feel I'm not a nice guy which is not true, but I wasn't overlooked. I finished second. I could have finished fourth. You know what? Life goes on. I think expectations is the key word. People really expect an all-around performance from me."

As Darryl Strawberry approached the 1989 season, much was anticipated of him and the Mets. Darryl was coming off a great 1988 season. Most experts favored the Mets to win the Eastern Division championship. Darryl could not have prepared for what turned out to be a season filled with injuries and disappointments.

Baseball has its ups and downs.

Despite hitting twenty-nine homers and driving in seventy-seven runs, Darryl's performance at the plate was not up to his usual standards. He never gained consistent confidence with his bat, hitting a professional low of .225. However, he did average a home run every 16.4 at-bats. Darryl was also slowed by a foot injury. He played in just 134 games and stole only eleven bases.

Darryl had more than his own performance to worry about. The team lacked stability. Darryl and the Mets were forced to adjust to the coming and going of teammates. The Mets rarely had a set lineup. In addition, with the exception of infielder Howard Johnson, the Mets received little offensive support. Slowed by age and injuries, Mets stars and co-captains Gary Carter and Keith Hernandez produced sub-par years. With this unexpected turn of events, Carter and Hernandez offered the team little protection. With only the offensive support of Johnson and Strawberry, the Mets were forced to rely on their pitching staff. However, the Mets never scored enough runs to pose a serious challenge for the Eastern Division title. As a result, the Mets only finished in second place in the pennant race, six games behind the Eastern Division champion Chicago Cubs. The year ended on an even lower note as the Mets management released several of the players and coaches, among them Carter and Hernandez, from the ball club.

The season also brought some trying times for Darryl off the field. He and his wife Lisa decided they would get a divorce. Then they changed their minds.

Darryl's personal troubles surfaced again in early 1990. Strawberry entered the Smithers Center in Manhattan to treat an alcohol problem. Facing his own shortcomings helped Darryl try to improve himself. Now he had the opportunity to strengthen his performance on the baseball diamond as well.

Out of the Smithers Center, Darryl rejoined the Mets for the 1990 season. The Mets and their fans hoped for a "new

Darryl Strawberry." Frank Cashen, the general manager said "Darryl looks good and he feels great. It's just a question of can he continue his recovery." However, Darryl's season start was a disappointment. After the first six weeks of the season, his average was a mediocre .235 and he hit only four homers.

Then Davey Johnson, the Mets' manager, was replaced with Bud Harrelson. Almost overnight, Strawberry began an eighteen-game hitting streak. Darryl continued to perform well through the season and was chosen once again to be on the National League All-Star team.

At the same time, Darryl was in the middle of yet another controversy. With his contract expiring at the end of the season, teams like the Dodgers and the Cardinals began to inquire about him. The baseball commissioner raised tampering charges, but nothing ever materialized. Players are not allowed to talk with other teams until the season ends.

On June 27, Darryl stated he'd like to stay with the Mets. But then, in the middle of the season, negotiations with the Mets fell through. Darryl wanted a long-range deal similar to the five-year $23.5 million contract Jose Canseco signed with the Oakland Athletics. Mets management said they would take a chance on losing him to another team, and wait until the end of the season to renew negotiations.

A feud between the Mets and the Philadelphia Phillies that began in 1989 came to a head in a twenty-minute brawl on August 7. Strawberry, Tim Teufel, Dwight Gooden, three Phillies, and Phillies Coach Mike Ryan were all expelled from the game and later fined.

With two weeks left in the season Darryl suffered a back injury that kept him from playing in seven crucial games. The Mets finished the 1990 season four games out of first place in the Eastern Division with 91 wins and 71 losses. Darryl placed second in the National League homers race with 37.

Now, Darryl had to make a decision about where he would be playing the next season. It had been known for some time that Darryl would like to play in his hometown of Los Angeles. Strawberry had a dream of playing with his buddies Eric Davis and Chris Brown.

Darryl's dream came true on November 7, 1990. He signed a five-year $20.25 million contract with the Dodgers. Darryl's dream of playing for the Dodgers was no joke—he reportedly passed up a higher offer from another team.

Now he was set to repeat his successes—in Los Angeles. Although his hitting would most likely be as strong as ever, he was to play centerfield. Darryl's strength is as a rightfielder. As a centerfielder he would have to field both sides.

Darryl's accomplishments have been many. He has had eight straight seasons with twenty-six or more home runs. He was the first National Leaguer to be picked as starter in the All-Star game for his first six full seasons in the majors. Darryl is the only National Leaguer to have twenty homers and twenty stolen bases each season in his first five full seasons. He set a Mets record with thirty-nine homers in one season and was New York's career home run leader with 223.

In 1991, Darryl played his first season for the Dodgers and had another excellent season. He hit 28 home runs and had 99 RBIs as the Dodgers finished in second place, behind the Atlanta Braves.

The next year was the beginning of a series of seasons filled with either physical or personal problems for Strawberry. In 1992, Darryl suffered a back injury that caused him to miss most of the 1992 and 1993 seasons.

At the start of the 1994 exhibition season Darryl's back was healthy and he seemed to be committed to having an All-Star caliber season. He later admitted to having a drug problem, and that he needed to seek treatment. The Dodgers cut him from the team. In June, after completing a drug treatment program, he was signed by the San Francisco Giants. He finished the season with the Giants, and hoped to become a starting outfielder in the upcoming year.

The next year turned out to be another lost season for Strawberry. On January 28, 1995, he was found guilty of not paying his taxes and on February 6, 1995, he was suspended by Major League Baseball for sixty days for failing another drug test. After his suspension was over, the New York Yankees took a chance and signed Strawberry for the remainder of the season. He played in thirty-two games for the Yankees, but more importantly he did not have any more drug problems.

Darryl started off the 1996 season in the minor leagues. On July 4, he signed with the Yankees once again. He was to provide the team with power from the left side of the plate. He did just that. He hit 11 home runs in 63 games, helping guide the Yankees to a first place finish. Then, in the American League Championship Series he hit 3 home runs in five games, as the Yankees defeated the Baltimore Orioles. The Yankees then went on to win the World Series, beating the Atlanta Braves in six games.

Strawberry started the 1997 season as the Yankees starting leftfielder. Unfortunately, pain in his left knee kept him out of action for most of the year.

Strawberry started off well in 1998, and led the Yankees in home runs for most of the season. He finished with 24 homers, his most since 1991. The Yankees had one of the best seasons in baseball history, finishing the year 114–48. Strawberry was unable to finish out the year. Just before the start of the postseason, Strawberry was diagnosed with colon cancer and had to undergo surgery. His battle with cancer was an inspiration to his teammates. They wore his number on their uniforms as they swept the San Diego Padres to win the 1998 World Series.

In the offseason, the treatments for Strawberry's cancer were working well. He hoped to join the Yankees sometime in the 1999 season. Then, Strawberry made another mistake. He was arrested in Tampa, Florida. The police said that they had found cocaine in his wallet. Strawberry was suspended once more, and is hoping for another chance to play baseball.

Career Statistics

YEAR	CLUB	G	AB	R	H	2B	3B	HR	RBI	SB	AVG
1983	Mets	122	420	63	108	15	7	26	74	19	.257
1984	Mets	147	522	75	131	27	4	26	97	27	.251
1985	Mets	111	393	78	109	15	4	29	79	26	.277
1986	Mets	136	475	76	123	27	5	27	93	28	.259
1987	Mets	154	532	108	151	32	5	39	104	36	.284
1988	Mets	153	543	101	146	27	3	39	101	29	.269
1989	Mets	134	476	69	107	26	1	29	77	16	.225
1990	Mets	152	542	92	150	18	1	37	108	15	.277
1991	Dodgers	139	505	86	134	22	4	28	99	10	.265
1992	Dodgers	43	156	20	37	8	0	5	25	3	.237
1993	Dodgers	32	100	12	14	2	0	5	12	1	.140
1994	Giants	29	92	13	22	3	1	4	17	0	.239
1995	Yankees	32	87	15	24	4	1	3	13	0	.276
1996	Yankees	63	202	35	53	13	0	11	36	6	.262
1997	Yankees	11	29	1	3	1	0	0	2	0	.103
1998	Yankees	101	295	44	73	11	2	24	57	8	.247
TOTALS		1,559	5,369	888	1,385	251	38	332	994	224	.258

G=Games   H=Hits   **HR**=Home Runs   **AVG**=Batting average
AB=At Bats   **2B**=Doubles   **RBI**=Runs Batted In
R=Runs   **3B**=Triples   **SB**=Stolen Bases

Where to Write Darryl Strawberry

Mr. Darryl Strawberry
c/o New York Yankees
Yankee Stadium
Bronx, NY 10451

On the Internet at: http://204.202.129.20/mlb/profiles/profile/3216.html

Index